TABLE TALK
WITH JESUS

TABLE TALK WITH JESUS

KENNETH L. MAULDIN

Abingdon
Nashville

TABLE TALK WITH JESUS

Copyright © 1979 by Abingdon

All rights reserved.
No part of this book may be reproduced in any manner
whatsoever without written permission of the publisher
except brief quotations embodied in critical articles
or reviews. For information address Abingdon,
Nashville, Tennessee

Library of Congress Cataloging in Publication Data

MAULDIN, KENNETH, 1918-
Table talk with Jesus.

1. Bible. N.T. Luke—Sermons. 2. Presbyterian
Church—Sermons. 3. Sermons, American. I. Title.
ISBN 0-687-40820-2

The Scripture quotations in this publication are from the Revised
Standard Version Common Bible, copyrighted © 1973 by the
Division of Christian Education of the National Council of the
Churches of Christ in the U.S.A., and are used by permission.

Scripture quotations noted NEB are from The New English Bible. ©
the Delegates of the Oxford University Press and the Syndics of the
Cambridge University Press 1961, 1970. Reprinted by permission.

The Scripture quotation noted Phillips is from The New Testament
in Modern English, copyright © J. B. Phillips 1958, 1960, 1972.

MANUFACTURED BY THE PARTHENON PRESS AT
NASHVILLE, TENNESSEE, UNITED STATES OF AMERICA

I dedicate this volume to the First Presbyterian Church of Topeka, Kansas. No pastor could preach to a more responsive and appreciative congregation. They challenge me to do my best. Again and again this beloved congregation has confirmed my conviction that a series of biblically based, related sermons sustains interest and builds attendance.

The church has no substitute for preaching. In the context of prayer and worship, the sermon can become—and through the miracle of God's grace sometimes does become—the Word of God spoken. A sermon can only become the Word of God spoken when it is heard. I express gratitude to all those who listen so carefully and thereby make miracles possible!

Contents

Foreword

I am proud to say that I know this author; he is my pastor. Sitting in a pew before him in our beautiful church, my wife and I have heard these sermons and many others. We rejoice that more people will now be able to read them.

One of the ways we communicate with one another is through the convention of dining, that is, eating together with a degree of formality. As food goes into our mouths, vocal sounds—words and laughter—go into our ears, and pleasant sights greet our eyes. It is a ceremony around a provision for sustenance; it is a mutual communication and a pledge of friendship. In conversation we delicately probe the state of our relationships. We associate with the pleasure of the meal the exchange of messages and reassurances. It is a very human ceremony.

As Dr. Mauldin read over the accounts of Jesus dining with people, he was thinking of this total meaning. He tried to imagine just what might have been said at those historical meals beyond the words recorded. He reflected, I am sure, that there must have been many other dinings and suppings together and many communications between teacher and disciples to which we are not privy. Dr. Mauldin gives us a chance to play with the picture of Jesus with his friends (and others!), adding our own extrapolations.

This he often does when he preaches, and we listen and learn.

You can see why we like to hear him and why we are glad you can hear him through this book. You will detect his great sincerity, his thoughtfulness and reverence, and perhaps you too will begin to share silently in some dinner conversations with the Teacher.

Karl Menninger, M.D.
Topeka

Preface

Our fascination with Jesus of Nazareth never ends. Part of this fascination is due to our knowledge that when "lifted up," Jesus draws to Himself people of greatly different interests, concerns, and cultures. To rebels, Jesus is a revolutionary. To lovers of peace, He is the Prince of Peace. To the brokenhearted, He is the man of sorrows, acquainted with grief. To the sick, He is the Great Physician who binds up their wounds and heals their diseases. To the enslaved, He is the Liberator who sets prisoners free. To the humanist, He is perfect man, a reflection of what human flesh should be: the Son of man. To the theologian, He is "very God of very God," the express image of the Father: the Son of God.

The four Gospels give us the only authentic picture we have of Jesus, though the balance of the New Testament continues to interpret the meaning of his mission and message. Distinctions have been made between the Jesus of history and the Christ of faith, but stressing these distinctions creates distortions. Our faith is anchored in history, and the New Testament is needed both for inspiration and correction. I remind myself of the time as a teen-ager when I first heard Jesus described by His critical contemporaries as "a glutton and a winebibber" (cf. Luke 7:34 and Matt. 11:19 KJV). Comfortable conceptions of Jesus as the One who went about "doing good," teaching, preaching, and healing, had to be enlarged to take into account the fact that Jesus also enjoyed good food and pleasant company! I also remember

11

listening to those who found fault because the Gospels did not express enough social concern. How can anyone read the Gospels without seeing that racism, segregation, discrimination, and prejudice were intolerable to Jesus? As affronts to human dignity He hit them hard and often. And His disciples, once they had His mind and shared His spirit, also became passionate advocates of human rights. For them, too, the barriers of race and class came down. "God has shown me," said Peter, "that I should not call any man common or unclean" (Acts 10:28).

The apostle Paul said that Jesus was God's "inexpressible gift" to the world (cf. II Cor. 9:15); and that he had been given the grace to preach to the Gentiles "the unsearchable riches of Christ" (Eph. 3:8).

To wander through the stacks of a modern theological library and glance at row after row after row of volumes that relate to Jesus—His life, His message, His mission, His offices, His glory—is to know that He is too big, too great, for any individual mind to comprehend. He is God's inexpressible gift; yet speak of Him we must!

I shall be pleased if this slender volume exalts the name of Jesus and encourages people to read Luke's witness to him as the Savior who "receives sinners and eats with them" (Luke 15:1).

I express personal appreciation to Mrs. Margaret Guffey, a patient and competent secretary, whose typewriter makes fewer mistakes than mine!

I. Matthew's Motley Crew

Scripture: After this he went out, and saw a tax collector, named Levi, sitting at the tax office; and he said to him, "Follow me." And he left everything, and rose and followed him.

And Levi made him a great feast in his house; and there was a large company of tax collectors and others sitting at table with them. And the Pharisees and their scribes murmured against his disciples, saying, "Why do you eat and drink with tax collectors and sinners?" And Jesus answered them, "Those who are well have no need of a physician, but those who are sick; I have not come to call the righteous, but sinners to repentance."

And they said to him, "The disciples of John fast often and offer prayers, and so do the disciples of the Pharisees, but yours eat and drink."

And Jesus said to them, "Can you make wedding guests fast while the bridegroom is with them? The days will come, when the bridegroom is taken away from them, and then they will fast in those days." He told them a parable also: "No one tears a piece from a new garment and puts it upon an old garment; if he does, he will tear the new, and the piece from the new will not match the old. And no one puts new wine into old wineskins; if he does, the new wine will burst the skins and it will be spilled, and the skins will be destroyed. But new wine must be put into fresh wineskins.

And no one after drinking old wine desires new; for he says, 'The old is good.' " (Luke 5:27-39)

I

The Gospel of Luke has more stories concerning Jesus at mealtime than the other Gospels. There are reasons for this. It would be no accident for Luke to be especially interested in the table talk of Jesus and in events that happened when Jesus was in various homes. Luke was a Gentile and, so far as we know, the only Gentile writer of any part of the New Testament. His Gospel, and his history of the early church, known to us as *The Acts of the Apostles,* represent a considerable part of the New Testament; but even so, as a Greek physician it would be inevitable for him to see Jesus with the eyes of a Gentile. To recall how exclusive the Jewish people were as far as table fellowship with Gentiles was concerned suggests that Luke would deeply appreciate the fact that his beloved master was a friend of sinners who without hesitation sat at table, and ate and drank, with all who invited Him, whether they were hated Jewish tax collectors or Gentile sinners or others considered by the orthodox religious to be beyond the bounds of God's concern. This openness on the part of Jesus, this acceptance of others, this rebellion against existing social and religious barriers, would be special reason for Luke to love Jesus.

Luke proclaimed the gospel—the good news of God's love for all men—by using the table talk of Jesus and the events that happened when people shared dinner with Him.

II

The first dinner scene reported by Luke takes place in the home of the tax collector Levi.

Jesus had seen Levi at the tax office and had invited him to leave his tax collecting and follow Him as a disciple. So briefly and matter-of-factly is Levi's call reported that it is easy to miss its high significance. The importance magnifies once we realize that the call of only half of the Twelve is reported at all. Levi's call was especially important because he was a social and religious outcast. Matthew's call is a favorite subject in stained-glass windows.

Levi and Matthew are the same. In Palestine it was quite customary for men to have two names because most people used two languages: Greek and Aramaic. The universally understood name, and the one used in business, would be their Greek name. Within the family, or in more intimate circles, the Aramaic would be used. The name "Matthew" means "the Gift of God," and it is entirely possible that Jesus gave Levi this name when he became a disciple, just as He gave Simon the new name of "Peter" when he was called. Since Luke was a Gentile, it would be typical for him to use the Greek name.

All thanks to Doctor Luke for telling us that first off Matthew entertains Jesus and His disciples with a banquet at his house. To honor Jesus, and to introduce Him to his friends, must have been Matthew's intent.

He had many friends, but all were tax collectors and sinners, like himself.

In Matthew's spontaneous, joyful response to Jesus, could he have understood the full dimension of his actions? Jesus had accepted him, had asked him to become a disciple; and he had responded. Now nothing could ever be the same again. The significance of that dinner with Matthew's motley crew would not escape Luke, because he himself had known what it feels like to be excluded, to be looked down upon, to feel the silent pains of social ostracism.

By this time in Palestine the words "tax collector" and "publican" were virtually synonymous. It had not always been so. *"Publicanus"* was a Latin word, and originally it applied to a man engaged in public service. Gradually the meaning centered in on those who handled public funds, especially taxes. No class of men were so detested by Jews as the renegade Jews who collected taxes for the despised Romans. No respectable Jew would accept such employment. Those who did were treated as the dregs of society. Their word was not accepted in courts of law. They were banned from synagogue worship. They were considered on a par with murderers and robbers. Such heated attitudes were inflamed by religious convictions, because to a strict Jew tribute should be paid to none save God. To pay tribute to anyone else was to compromise loyalty to God. This was the issue behind the test put to Jesus about whether or not tribute should be paid to Caesar. Likewise, Jesus' parable about the Pharisee and the publican praying in the temple reminds us that the publican knew he was not welcome there. Perhaps he had hoped to find the temple empty; but so great was his personal distress, that he could not leave without prayer, even if a Pharisee was there. He stands "far off." He will not even lift up his eyes to heaven. He beats his breast, saying, "God, be merciful to me a sinner!" (Luke 18:13).

It is nothing short of astonishing that Jesus should ever call a man like Matthew, and just as astonishing that Matthew should accept. Something higher and sturdier than the walls of Jericho were tumbling down! Luke wants us to hear the rumble and the roar of tumbling walls. "Why do you eat and drink with tax collectors and sinners?"—this was the anguished, angry question of religious people. Jesus' quiet reply would make Luke's heart pound with proud excitement: "Those who are well have no need of a physician, but those who are sick; I have not come to call the righteous, but sinners to repentance" (vv. 30, 31).

This revolutionary answer sounds so simple and so authentic and so reasonable that our temptation is to say, "Of course! Naturally! What else? Who could honor a doctor so fearful of infection and contagion that he flees all who are ill and associates only with the healthy?"

Yet how easy it has always been for religious people to justify standing apart from those who need acceptance and love and forgiveness, and to defend their separation in the name of purity. One mark of religious demagoguery is to quote scripture out of context, saying: "Come ye apart. Be ye separate. Don't associate with dogs, nor cast your pearls before swine. Minister to your own kind. Forget about those sinners. They deserve what they'll get!"

How thankful we should be that Jesus accepted Matthew and his motley crew, and ate and drank with them, and defended them before those who counted them as refuse. Who but Jesus could have guessed that a publican could ever become an apostle, or that fishermen could become prophets, or that ordinary people could ever hope to share the banquet table of heaven? And how essential it is that the church, which bears Christ's name, do everything in its power to maintain the same catholicity of spirit, to avoid harsh and judgmental attitudes, to remember that under the tutelage of Jesus even a Matthew could become a hero of the faith!

III

Those reprimanded now reprimand in turn. Jesus and His disciples are criticized for not being pious enough. They eat, and they drink. Where are the sacred disciplines? The marks of holiness are not on them. To Jesus they say, "The disciples of John fast often and offer prayers, and so do the disciples of the Pharisees, but yours eat and drink" (v. 33).

This charge was not frivolous. A serious response is deserved. Surely there is a legitimate place for self-discipline and for regular religious observances!

Prayer is as natural as breathing. Fasting is a normal expression of sorrow. Prayer is friendship with God.

In contrition or need we may say: "I'm not hungry. I'd rather not eat just now." But there are those who would systematize prayer and fasting, like so many other natural human emotions and responses, and value them for some ulterior good, and then be proud of their somber sacrifices. And often those most rigorous about self-discipline are the very ones who resent or envy or even despise those who live in greater freedom because the same disciplines and agonies are not freely chosen by all. He was a wise counselor who said to a young pastor in training, "Sir, don't make an agony of your religion!"

With a simple analogy, Jesus turned aside the criticism of His seemingly irreligious conduct. "Can you make wedding guests fast while the bridgroom is with them? The days will come, when the bridegroom is taken away from them, and then they will fast in those days" (vv. 34, 35).

It was not uncommon for wedding celebrations in Palestine to last a week. It was not their custom for young people to leave home for a honeymoon. They stayed in their own village, perhaps even in the home of one of the parents, but for a whole week they kept open house. They were treated as a king and queen, and they dressed the part. Sometimes they even wore crowns, and for one whole week of their lives their word was law. By common consent all members of the wedding party were exempt from work, and from all religious duties, such as fasting, because these might interfere with the general merriment. Guests sharing this festive week were called children of the bridechamber, and bride and groom and guests alike

19

lived such a joyful week that all the drabness of other weeks was forgotten.

By reporting Jesus' defense of His apparently irreligious behavior, Luke was also testifying to his faith that Jesus was the Messiah and that with the coming of Jesus the kingdom also came. Luke reports Jesus as saying that if fasting is out of place during a wedding, how much more out of place it is now that the kingdom of God has arrived!

The walls of Jericho were falling! Barriers that had separated men for so long were crashing down. Yes, there was rumble and roar; but how sad that so quickly the meaning gets distorted. It will not be long, believe it or not, until this very word from Jesus will be interpreted by the church as justifying fasting! "See," they will say, "the bridegroom has been taken from us. We must fast all the more!" Then two brief parables get attached to the story of this meal scene, and the meaning of these parables is not completely clear. The meaning at first seems clear enough. New wine requires new wineskins. Old religious forms cannot hold this new kingdom being brought by Jesus. His new and radical demands cannot be patched upon old garments. New patches don't match old cloth. New wine bursts and destroys old skins. That seems clear enough until we read, "And no one after drinking old wine desires new; for he says, 'The old is good' " (v. 39).

What is being said here? Is the old being commended, or is this the simple recognition that there was good in the old and it will always be tempting to be content with it? Is the accent still on the warning not to expect old forms to contain the new? I think so. And we who share a Christian heritage, and who therefore think we know what the new wine is, are the very ones who need to be warned, lest we imagine that the forms we know, and the order we know and cherish, are to be permanent. Perhaps it should be put this way: if we are unyielding in our loyalty to Christ Jesus, then we can afford to keep an open mind on all else, and strive to keep life open for the surprises of the Holy Spirit. As disciples of Jesus, we should live joyfully in the freedom He gives us, living to the full, eating and drinking with all others who rejoice that the kingdom has come, even to such a motley crew as we be. Amen.

II. Love in Action

Scripture: One of the Pharisees asked him to eat with him, and he went into the Pharisee's house, and took his place at table. And behold, a woman of the city, who was a sinner, when she learned that he was at table in the Pharisee's house, brought an alabaster flask of ointment, and standing behind him at his feet, weeping, she began to wet his feet with her tears, and wiped them with the hair of her head, and kissed his feet, and anointed them with the ointment. Now when the Pharisee who had invited him saw it, he said to himself, "If this man were a prophet, he would have known who and what sort of woman this is who is touching him, for she is a sinner." And Jesus answering said to him, "Simon, I have something to say to you." And he answered, "What is it, Teacher?" "A certain creditor had two debtors; one owed five hundred denarii, and the other fifty. When they could not pay, he forgave them both. Now which of them will love him more?" Simon answered, "The one, I suppose, to whom he forgave more." And he said to him, "You have judged rightly." Then turning toward the woman he said to Simon, "Do you see this woman? I entered your house, you gave me no water for my feet, but she has wet my feet with her tears and wiped them with her hair. You gave me no kiss, but from the time I came in she has not ceased to kiss my feet. You did not anoint my head with oil, but she has anointed my feet with ointment. Therefore I tell you, her sins, which are many, are forgiven, for she loved much; but he who is forgiven little, loves little." And he said to her, "Your sins are forgiven." Then those who were at table with him began to say among themselves, "Who is this, who even forgives sin?" And he said to the woman, "Your faith has saved you; go in peace." (Luke 7:36-50)

I

The openness of Jesus, His rebellion against the social and religious barriers of His day, His willingness to accept, and to identify with, the sinners and tax collectors and the poor, would all be special reasons for Luke, a Gentile physician, to love Jesus. Jews at that time were very exclusive as far as table fellowship with others was concerned; so in writing his Gospel, Luke used the meal scenes and the table talk of Jesus to tell the good news of a love that overturned barriers separating people from one another.

The first dinner scene reported by Luke took place in the home of Matthew, the tax collector. Matthew's friends were there—a motley crew of tax collectors and sinners—but it was a dramatic way of showing Jesus' acceptance of a man who was a social and religious outcast. That story is told in the fifth chapter. In the seventh chapter the focus of attention is upon a woman who was a social, religious, and moral outcast. The drama of this dinner is intensified by the fact that it takes place in the home of a Pharisee, one of the Separated Ones, a man whose life was dedicated to holiness. How terrible that Jesus, a Jew, should enter the house of a publican and eat the food and drink the wine of a renegade Jew, despised by Pharisees as scum of the earth and the dregs of society. There was nothing wrong, however, in a Pharisee inviting a wandering rabbi to his home for dinner.

II

There are three principal characters in the drama of this dinner scene, and Luke wants us to look closely and listen carefully as each acts and speaks. First, there is the Pharisee, the host, whose name we learn is Simon. Second, the guest: Jesus. Third, an unnamed woman of the streets. Tradition keeps trying to give her a name, but there is no reason for identifying her as Mary Magdalene or any other Mary. Perhaps the drama is more meaningful with her name unknown.

Only hints are given as to why Simon should invite Jesus to dinner. His motives are not clear. Perhaps it was curiosity or genuine interest or an opportunity to find fault.

Picture the scene in your imagination. At that time in Palestine the homes of well-to-do people were built around open courtyards. The courtyard would be a pleasant place, with trees and a garden, possibly a fountain. In pleasant weather it would be a happy place to entertain and to serve meals.

Those kind enough to invite a traveling rabbi or teacher to their home for a meal acquired both religious merit and social prestige, especially if their guest had spoken that day in the local synagogue. And strange as it may seem to us, all sorts of people—

friends, neighbors, acquaintances—were quite free to wander in and out of the courtyard. It would be flattering to the host if several people from the neighborhood should come to listen quietly to the pious wisdom and nimble wit of a distinguished rabbi. And the more people who came to listen, the more complimented the host. This may explain why the unnamed woman would be free to enter the courtyard.

Customs of that time dictated that at least three courtesies should be extended a guest. The host would greet his guest by placing his right hand on the guest's shoulder and giving him the kiss of peace. For a distinguished rabbi this gesture of respect would never be omitted. Then, because the streets were dusty, and sandals were leather pads held in place by straps, it was easy to leave one's sandals at the door. But cool water was available to be poured over the guest's feet, both to cleanse and to comfort. Then a small amount of sweet-smelling oil was placed on the guest's head. Not one of these courtesies was extended to Jesus, though good manners would demand nothing less. What sort of a man was this Simon anyway?

It begins to appear that Simon was a discourteous snob who invited Jesus to dinner either to embarrass Him with patronizing contempt or to attract attention to himself for entertaining one whose reputation for revolutionary behavior was spreading far and wide.

Simon is preoccupied with his study of Jesus, watching every expression of His face, when the third character of this courtyard drama appears. A woman

25

of soiled reputation, known and talked about by most of the men and women of the village, heard that Jesus was at dinner in the Pharisee's house. She comes up behind Him and kneels at His feet.

In the east people did not sit at table, as we do. They reclined on low couches, resting on the left elbow, leaving the right arm and hand free for serving themselves. A low table with food on it would be in the center, and guests could reach the food from their couch. If Jesus was thus reclining on the couch, resting on His elbow, with feet stretched out behind, His position explains how this woman could be kneeling at His feet unobserved. It was also customary for Jewish women to wear around their neck a little flask carved from alabaster stone, containing a concentrated perfume. Sometimes these flasks were almost translucent, like glass, or were beautifully banded with diffused colors. They were expensive, prized possessions.

Now, back to the drama! Impulsively this woman opens her alabaster of perfume and empties all of it on Jesus' feet. Then tears come like a flood—costly tears mingled with costly perfume. Then, as though unaware that anyone would see, she unbinds her long hair and tries to wipe His feet. It was an act of gravest immodesty for a woman to unbind her hair in the presence of men, but so overcome with emotion is this woman that the impropriety of her actions seem not to matter, for she continues to wet His feet with tears, and then to kiss, and then to wipe again with her hair. Ineffective, blinded actions, but actions laden with emotion. A more dramatic tribute can scarcely be imagined!

Now it is that Simon says to himself, "If this fellow were a prophet, he would know what kind of woman this is who keeps touching him, for she is a bad woman!"

Now, Simon, the more we hear about you the less we like you! You are a good man, a religious man, and we do not question that once upon a time your greatest desire was to live a life pleasing to God; but, Simon, something has gone wrong, terribly wrong, when religious people are so quick to criticize and categorize and become judgmental. Your cynical prejudice against Jesus is immediately confirmed; without hesitation you brand this brokenhearted woman a sinful prostitute. Whether you know it or not, Simon, you shut yourself off from the God of love and mercy because, in your own mind, you don't need mercy and in your eyes you have done nothing requiring forgiveness. How blind self-righteousness becomes, Simon—how blind, how blind!

Jesus said to him, "Simon, I have something to say to you." And Simon answered, "What is it, Teacher?" "Two men were in debt to the same moneylender. One owed five hundred dollars; the other, fifty. Since neither could repay him, he generously canceled both debts. Which one do you suppose will love him more?"

Have you noticed how Jesus often used money —and the use people make of it—to reveal our deepest motivations? We say money is only a medium of exchange. It is always more, of course. Few windows into personality are more revealing than the way money is handled, both in the acquiring of it and

27

the expending of it. Marriage counselors sometimes use the study of a family's finances to reveal to marriage partners the concealed images they have of themselves and of their children. Here Jesus used money as a way of talking about forgiveness and love.

But let's not get hung up with Simon, nor linger over the obvious sins of self-righteousness. We shall not see love in action, nor hear the gospel of confession and forgiveness, until we see the third person in this drama and hear her sobbing.

What do we really know about her? Nothing much, really. In simplest fashion she is described as "a woman of the city, . . . a sinner" (v. 37).

Why does she kneel at Jesus' feet? Why does she weep?

Love and forgiveness are never far apart. No one is nearer God than a sinner who repents. Was she driven to see Jesus because of His reputation as a revolutionary prophet who treated women as full-fledged persons worthy of respect, never jeering at them for being female nor ridiculing them as inferior? The first words of chapter 8 are explosive in the context of that society. I quote: "Soon afterward he [Jesus] went on through cities and villages, preaching and bringing the good news of the kingdom of God. And the twelve were with him, and also some women who had been healed of evil spirits and infirmities: Mary, called Magdalene, from whom seven demons had gone out, and Joanna, the wife of Chuza, Herod's steward, and Susanna, and many others, who provided for them out of their means" (8:1-3). This is incredible! Talk about revolutionary! When before had any rabbi included women among his disciples? The prestigious modern Jewish scholar Joachim Jeremias writes in *New Testament Theology* that to include women as Jesus did was an unprecedented happening in the history of that time. Nor were these just poor, rootless women whose lives had been renewed by His understanding concern. They included such well-to-do women as Joanna, wife of the steward of King Herod Antipas, and Susanna—women of means who helped provide for the needs of the whole group who went about with Jesus. News of a prophet who brushed aside the barriers of religious caste and sex and prejudice, and treated everyone with equal concern, would spread like wildfire—even without T.V. and radio! Small wonder that women wept when they saw Jesus carrying His own cross through the streets of Jerusalem! They had reason. He had been their advocate, their strong champion. His acceptance of them set them free and made them whole.

Now, let's be clear about the meaning of this parable. Nothing here indicates that Jesus took lightly this woman's tears, or that He dismissed her sins as nothing. His parable is misinterpreted if we think He recommends sin so that God may pardon. This is blasphemous. It is her love that is heralded, not her misdeeds; it is her consciousness of sin, not her sin, that is commended. Her love did not *earn* her forgiveness. She was forgiven but not because she wept. Tears can be bitter, or tears can cleanse. Tears do not save; faith does. Faith forces her to her knees at Jesus' feet.

29

III. When Self-Concern Controls

Scripture: Now as they went on their way, he entered a village; and a woman named Martha received him into her house. And she had a sister called Mary, who sat at the Lord's feet and listened to his teaching. But Martha was distracted with much serving; and she went to him and said, "Lord, do you not care that my sister has left me to serve alone? Tell her then to help me." But the Lord answered her, "Martha, Martha, you are anxious and troubled about many things; one thing is needful. Mary has chosen the good portion, which shall not be taken away from her." (Luke 10:38-42)

I

Luke, a Gentile physician, must have been especially proud that Jesus, whom he loved so much, did not exclude Himself from table fellowship with Gentiles, publicans, sinners, and others socially unacceptable to religious purists. By eating and drinking with all sorts and conditions of people Jesus identified with them, acting out, as it were, His commission to preach the gospel of the kingdom of God to the poor, the captives, the blind, and the oppressed (cf. Luke 4:18). Luke reports the contemptuous charge repeatedly brought against Jesus: "This man receives sinners and eats with them" (Luke 15:2).

One or two modern interpreters have reasoned that Jesus used this approach to the poor, the weak, and the helpless as a strategy, a way of mobilizing disinherited people in His own game of power politics, to use them as a lever against vested power structures. This theory is interesting, perhaps; but it just won't hold up. By picking and choosing their evidence, these interpreters reinterpret the New Testament in distorted contemporary terms. Just now it is popular with a few "liberationists" to interpret Jesus as a social and political revolutionary who was on the way toward overturning the society of His day, but unfortunately made a tragic mistake or two and got Himself crucified.

Thorough, objective study of the New Testament doesn't permit us to interpret Jesus as a folk hero who mobilized people for His own purposes. Actually, He was always pointing away from Himself, saying, "Your faith has saved you" (Luke 7:50); "See that you say nothing to any one; but go, show yourself to the priest . . ." (Matt. 8:4); "Return to your home, and declare how much God has done for you" (Luke 8:39). At the peak of popularity when, as the Gospel of John says, "perceiving . . . that they were about to come and take him by force to make him king, Jesus withdrew again to the mountain by himself" (John 6:15). When the seventy returned from their king-dom-preaching mission, flushed with success, elated with achievements, they exclaimed, "Lord, even the

31

demons are subject to us in your name!" (Luke 10:17). "Do not rejoice," He said, "that the spirits are subject to you; but rejoice that your names are written in heaven" (v. 20). It is closer to truth to say that in Jesus, people discovered their own worth and identity. In Him they discovered themselves as real people in God's coming kingdom; and in the new life of God's kingdom—this community of faith—they discovered a worth in themselves that no ruler could take from them. Christ's victory with the poor, the weak, and the powerless—those from the highways and hedges (Luke 14:23)—was far more profound than the success or failure of power politics!

The first dinner reported was in the home of Matthew, a tax collector—a story told in chapter 5. Breaking bread and drinking wine with Matthew and his motley crew was a dramatic way of showing Jesus' acceptance of a man who was a social and religious outcast. The seventh chapter tells of a woman who was a social, religious, and moral outcast who knelt in faith at Jesus' feet in Simon's house. That compelling, intensely dramatic story commends this unnamed woman's faith, not her tears. It heralds her love, not her misdeeds. At the end of chapter 10, the brief story of a dinner at the home of Martha and her sister, Mary, is inserted. It seems such a pleasant interlude. How different from the next meal Luke will report, which will take place in the home of an unfriendly Pharisee, where hot words and angry arguments will bounce back and forth between Jesus and Pharisees and Scribes.

32

II

Chances are you remember the table talk in the home of these sisters and assume that Jesus complimented Mary and reprimanded Martha. If that's all you remember, or if you think that's the message of this dinner scene, then perhaps we'd best look closely and read carefully.

Few Gospel stories have been so persistently mishandled. People seem determined to make it Mary and Martha's story, with a halo around Mary's head and Martha as a sourpuss drudge. Luke's introductory sentence makes it plain that this is Martha's story: "A woman named Martha received him into her house. . . ." The push to idealize Mary and downgrade Martha has persisted through the centuries until today. In the Middle Ages this story was used to exalt the contemplative life above the active. Mary's "better choice," her concern for "spiritual" things, confirmed the superiority of monastic life over the crudities of common life. Pietists have wanted to identify this Mary with Mary Magdalene and credit her with passionate devotion to Jesus for having cured her of seven demons (cf. Luke 8:2). Today the great temptation is for women's liberationists to seize upon this story and say: "How beautiful! See, Jesus reprimanded that domestic drudge with her concern for pots and pans, and her distress with the duties of serving, and complimented Mary for sitting at His feet and engaging in intelligent conversation!" There is little doubt that intelligent Christianity is the most liberating power in life—for men as well as for women—but let's not weaken the case with superficial interpretations of Scripture!

The history of biblical interpretation is a fascinating discipline and an important one. Frequently, scholars use two words I shall now use simply because all of us should know and understand them. The words are "exegesis" and "eisegesis." They are Greek words. The first is a compound of *"ex,"* meaning "out," and *"hegeisthai,"* meaning "to lead or guide." Exegesis, therefore, means to draw out the meaning of Scripture, to guide in finding its basic, true, or original meaning. *"Eis"* means "into," and put with *"hegeisthai,"* to lead or guide, means the opposite of exegesis. Eisegesis is to read ideas and interpretations *into* Scripture—ideas not there. It has come to mean imposing our own ideas upon Scripture. Any Bible interpreter concerned with integrity keeps this distinction in mind and works hard to be honest in exegesis and, at the least, acknowledges what is being done when indulging in eisegesis.

So, if the message of this story for you is "My life is frantic. I rush about attempting too many things. Isn't it time I gave contemplation, prayer, and thoughtful quietness a new place in my life?"—if that's your need, well and good! Or if your response to this story is "Hurrah again for Jesus! In the synagogues at that time women were almost nonpersons. They sat apart with the children and the slaves. Ten men were required for a quorum. Women were not counted. In the Jerusalem Temple women could go as far as their court, no farther. The inner court was for men only.

34

Synagogue schools were not open to women. They could not study philosophy or law or history or writing in the academies. The Torah was not to be taught them, and some rabbis went so far as to warn against talking overmuch with women. So hurrah for Jesus! Liberator of women!"—if that's what this story says to you, well and good. But in honesty let's admit there is more eisegesis than exegesis in both these responses.

III

Then what is this story saying?

Use the qualifiers required by honesty, such as "it appears," or "a careful reading of the text indicates," or what have you; but then center in on the signal that this is Martha's story. She is the hostess, the central figure. The meal takes place, as Luke says, in her house. Second, listen carefully and see if the emphasis doesn't fall more on Jesus' defense of Mary to Martha rather than on a praising of Mary to the disparagement of Martha.

Martha was free from selfishness. Her concern was to please Jesus. Her concern was not her own pleasure—a fault that she thought she saw in Mary. The gentle reproof from Jesus was that she had permitted self-concern to get in control. The clue is her question: "Lord, do you not care that my sister has left me to serve alone? Tell her then to help me" (v. 40). There is nothing wrong with hard work; there is nothing wrong with unselfishness; there is nothing wrong with trying hard to serve other people, nothing wrong even with sacrifice, provided it be self-forget-ful. But when self-concern controls, and we begin feeling sorry for ourselves because we have so many duties and must work so hard and are required to be so unselfish and so sacrificial, then, suddenly, all the goodness of our good work is drained away, and we become a misery to ourselves and a tryanny to others.

Do you agree that the central issue here is self-concern? Perhaps you will, perhaps not; but this is the way I hear it. And when Jesus said, "Martha, Martha, you are anxious and troubled about many things; one thing is needful. Mary has chosen the good portion, which shall not be taken away from her," I hear these words spoken in fondest respect for Martha, while at the same time refusing to deprive Mary of the choice she has made.

The most emphatic word I hear in this story is the warning to all of us activist church members who get so caught up in all our good works, and then when others seem not to notice, or when they don't compliment us, or worse yet, when they don't pitch in to help us, then our self-concern makes us critical of them and martyrs to ourselves.

Self-concern is the spoiler. It spoils it all when parents say to children, "How hard we've worked and sacrificed for you to have a good life!" It spoils it all when Dad says, "I've worked like a slave so my family could eat well and have a roof over their heads!" It spoils it all when Mom says, "Nobody appreciates how much time it takes to keep a family fed and clothed and clean." It spoils it all when the preacher says, "Nobody will ever know how many demands

36

are made on my time and energy." It spoils it all when the faithful members of church say, "This church would fall apart if it weren't for us! Twenty-five percent of us do seventy-five percent of all the work, and all the giving, and all the serving, and all the singing, and everything else."

"Lord, why don't you tell those loafers to help us? You know how it is, Lord. Some people will use any excuse to avoid doing important things. Here I am just knocking myself out day after day, doing my best to please you. You know how I am, Lord! I never was one to shirk and when there's work to be done, I do my share, and then some; but it just burns me up when others don't carry their share of the load! I just can't stand these people who sit around all the time when there's so much to be done, and so many needs, and so many people are hurting, and I'm getting so tired—and they just sit there!"

I wouldn't know, but I suspect that even a mystic in a monastery, who sits at Jesus' feet every day, could spoil it all if he should say: "Do you think anyone has noticed how sweetly beautiful my smile is today? Really, it's true: I'm a much better Christian today than I was a year ago!"

Perhaps it is rather easy to let self-concern get in control!

IV. Hot Arguments and a Cold Dinner

Scripture: While he was speaking, a Pharisee asked him to dine with him; so he went in and sat at table. The Pharisee was astonished to see that he did not first wash before dinner. And the Lord said to him, "Now you Pharisees cleanse the outside of the cup and of the dish, but inside you are full of extortion and wickedness. You fools! Did not he who made the outside make the inside also? But give for alms those things which are within; and behold, everything is clean for you.

"But woe to you Pharisees! for you tithe mint and rue and every herb, and neglect justice and the love of God; these you ought to have done, without neglecting the others. Woe to you Pharisees! for you love the best seat in the synagogues and salutations in the market places. Woe to you! for you are like graves which are not seen, and men walk over them without knowing it."

One of the lawyers answered him, "Teacher, in saying this you reproach us also." And he said, "Woe to you lawyers also! for you load men with burdens hard to bear, and you yourselves do not touch the burdens with one of your fingers. Woe to you! for you build the tombs of the prophets whom your fathers killed. So you are witnesses and consent to the deeds of your fathers; for they killed them, and you build their tombs. Therefore also the Wisdom of God said, 'I will send them prophets and apostles, some of whom they will kill and persecute,' that the blood of all the prophets, shed from the foundation of the world, may be required of this generation, from the blood of Abel to the blood of Zechariah, who perished between the altar and the sanctuary. Yes, I tell you, it shall be required of this generation. Woe to you lawyers! for you have taken away the key of knowledge; you did not enter yourselves and you hindered those who were entering." (Luke 11:37-52)

I

Luke tells of an occasion when Jesus was invited to dine in the home of an unfriendly Pharisee. While Jesus was speaking—presumably while He was preaching—this Pharisee interrupts His preaching and invites Him to dine with him. It sounds as though the invitation was given in a discourteous, perhaps condescending manner. The surprise is that Jesus accepts such a rude invitation. Perhaps He accepted because it was rude! "While he was speaking, a Pharisee asked him to dine with him; so he went in and sat at table." The text doesn't tell whether food was ever served or eaten. If served, then it must have been a cold meal because the words got hot so fast! The impression is that a fierce argument develops almost immediately.

Studies have been made of the psychological significance of sitting at table and breaking bread and eating with others. Sharing food with another implies recognition of another as a person like one's self. Food is a basic necessity of life, and to share it is to establish a relationship with another human being that implies the recognition of mutual needs and perhaps even an equality of humanity, even social equality.

39

The refusal to eat with others is rooted in some strongly felt need for maintaining distance and separation from those socially or religiously unacceptable. Some people do refuse to eat at the same table with people of another race; some will not break bread with others of a different social class. I understand there was a day when, at family gatherings or Sunday dinners, the children were not served until the adults had eaten. Was this a way of saying that children were not sufficiently civilized to eat with adults?

In this meal scene, controversy begins when the Pharisee notices with astonishment that Jesus did not wash before dinner. The invitation may have been rude, condescending, even insulting; nevertheless Jesus accepted. He enters the man's house and sits at his table. True, fault was found with Him immediately, but a surface interpretation could be that Jesus overreacted. He blasted His host! And not His host alone, but all Pharisees as well. His words were so hot, in fact, that the religious teachers present—the scribes, or lawyers of religion, if you will—felt blasted too! One of them said, "Teacher, in saying this you reproach us also" (11:45). Furthermore, Jesus was just as inhospitable to the lawyers as He had been to His host. "You fools!" (11:40) He said of the Pharisees, and then three times He said "Woe to you" for doing thus and so. The scribes were not called fools, but three choice "woes" were spoken against them too.

Having dinner with Jesus was a rather risky adventure!

II

Before going further, it may be good to warn ourselves against seeking simple satisfactions out of rehearsing the sins of first-century Pharisees. Sometimes Christians identify first-century Pharisaism with present day Judaism—which is simply not fair! True, there has been, and continues to be, disagreement and distance between the synagogue and the church; but we should never be guilty of distorting the disagreement, nor fail to be diligent in seeking to bridge the distance with a genuine desire to understand, to appreciate, and to cherish a common heritage—a great and glorious heritage of faith in the true and living God, the Father Almighty, the King of the universe!

It may not be altogether accurate, but let us raise the possibility that if a portrait of a first-century Pharisee be drawn, and if we search for a contemporary reflection of him in religion, we would find that reflection in certain expressions of the Christian faith today as much as in certain expressions of orthodox Judaism. It is an interesting question. Few are qualified to answer, but the question is raised only to make us cautious about drawing parallels.

Perhaps, then, we should ask, just who were the Pharisees? They were Jewish laymen who took their religion seriously. They believed religion should relate to the whole of life, not just to Temple sacrifices or Sabbath observances or occasional celebrations. Being serious, dedicated men, they wanted the Laws of God to be applied to the whole range of human life.

You could call them the "puritan party" within Judaism. Their peak of prominence and power was reached during the second century before Christ. Because their great desire was to live before God as good and righteous and holy men, they felt it necessary to separate themselves more and more from all that would defile. Their name itself probably means "the separated ones." Their love of the synagogue and its worship was proverbial, and to keep God's laws, their passion.

III

If we listen to the hot words between Jesus and an unfriendly Pharisee in as calm and quiet and cool a fashion as we can, perhaps we shall hear in this controversy the conflict between two completely different conceptions of religion. The basic question is: What is true religion? The Pharisees answer one way; Jesus another. To the Pharisee, religion meant obedience to law. The trouble with this answer is that law produces a legal religion concentrating on conduct. Jesus said that if Pharisees were as concerned about cleansing their hearts as washing their hands, they would be better men. The conflict is between inner motivation and self-control, and outer control based on codes of conduct. Legal religion is concerned with regulating what we do, and the attempt often becomes superficial.

Do Christian people—church members—need to be reminded that inward purity controls outward conduct? Don't pin hopes on codes of conduct. They so easily become regulatory and superficial.

Another peculiarity of legal religion is that it concentrates on not doing wrong, rather than on active and positive goodness. Negative goodness means acquiring merit by not smoking, not dancing, not drinking, not playing cards—and not going with the girls who do!

The Pharisee was so concerned not to transgress any command that he built a margin of safety around each law so as to be sure he did not transgress. The law of tithing, for example, applied only to agricultural produce. Just to be sure he really and truly did tithe, he tithed his herb garden as well, which meant carefully counting out 10 percent of his mint, anise seed, cumin seed, and dill. Any time religion gets this finicky and this strung out on technicalities, then we have forgotten what true religion is all about, namely, our relationship with God.

To concentrate, on the other hand, on the great moral obligations, such as love of God and justice among men, inevitably leaves us humble. Why? Simply because we don't live up to these demands, and never can. While recognizing that the great moral obligations are always beyond our reach, let's also be careful not to use these obligations to club one another into feelings of guilt and failure. Minor pieties thrive on recognition. If others don't notice or applaud or tell God about our virtues, then we will. "God, I thank thee that I am not like other men. . . . I fast, . . . I pray . . . I give tithes . . ." (Luke 18:11, 12). The other extreme is when great moral obligations are used to manipulate. Religious leaders, unfortunately, sometimes use this technique. The world hunger problem is sometimes presented in this manner. That Americans are efficient food producers is no reason for them to be made to feel like miserable cads and heartless exploiters. Actually, we are a nation of idealists, ready and willing to help and give and share. Let the appeal, therefore, be to our willingness to share. Appeal to our self-interest, if necessary, but let us not be forced to say: "What miserable sinners we be. None under the sun are so bad as we!" That motivation may get results, but it leaves people mumbling something like, "Here, take my contribution; give me a tax deduction; then get off my back. Religion drives me up the wall!"

There are sparks aplenty from this controversy between Jesus and the unfriendly Pharisee to suggest a whole constellation of truths worthy of keenest attention. Let us continue to examine ourselves lest we be guilty of the sins we delight to find in others. Amen.

V. Debunking Popular Pieties

Scripture: One sabbath when he went to dine at the house of a ruler who belonged to the Pharisees, they were watching him. And behold, there was a man before him who had dropsy. And Jesus spoke to the lawyers and Pharisees, saying, "Is it lawful to heal on the sabbath, or not?" But they were silent. Then he took him and healed him, and let him go. And he said to them, "Which of you, having a son or an ox that has fallen into a well, will not immediately pull him out on a sabbath day?" And they could not reply to this.

Now he told a parable to those who were invited, when he marked how they chose the places of honor, saying to them, "When you are invited by any one to a marriage feast, do not sit down in a place of honor, lest a more eminent man than you be invited by him; and he who invited you both will come and say to you, 'Give place to this man,' and then you will begin with shame to take the lowest place. But when you are invited, go and sit in the lowest place, so that when your host comes he may say to you, 'Friend, go up higher'; then you will be honored in the presence of all who sit at table with you. For every one who exalts himself will be humbled, and he who humbles himself will be exalted."

He said also to the man who had invited him, "When you give a dinner or a banquet, do not invite your friends or your brothers or your kinsmen or rich neighbors, lest they also invite you in return, and you be repaid. But when you give a

45

feast, invite the poor, the maimed, the lame, the blind, and you will be blessed, because they cannot repay you. You will be repaid at the resurrection of the just."

When one of those who sat at table with him heard this, he said to him, "Blessed is he who shall eat bread in the kingdom of God!" But he said to him, "A man once gave a great banquet, and invited many; and at the time for the banquet he sent his servant to say to those who had been invited, 'Come; for all is now ready.' But they all alike began to make excuses. The first said to him, 'I have bought a field, and I must go out and see it; I pray you, have me excused.' And another said, 'I have bought five yoke of oxen, and I go to examine them; I pray you, have me excused.' And another said, 'I have married a wife, and therefore I cannot come.' So the servant came and reported this to his master. Then the householder in anger said to his servant, 'Go out quickly to the streets and lanes of the city, and bring in the poor and maimed and blind and lame.' And the servant said, 'Sir, what you commanded has been done, and still there is room.' And the master said to the servant, 'Go out to the highways and hedges, and compel people to come in, that my house may be filled. For I tell you, none of those men who were invited shall taste my banquet.' " (Luke 14:1-24)

I

Debunking popular pieties was precisely what Jesus was doing in all the sabbath-day table talk in the home of an important ruler who belonged to the Pharisees.

The first popular piety punctured was the distorted importance of sabbath keeping. Luke says Jesus cured a man suffering with dropsy. His illness was not the issue. The important fact is that he was cured on the sabbath. Healing was defined as work. Jesus healed on the sabbath; therefore He broke a law of God, as the Pharisees understood it. No matter that a distressed human being was cured. All that mattered was that again Jesus identified Himself as a breaker of sacred law. This was why "they were watching him." What would this fellow do next?

First-century Pharisaism suffered an astonishing imbalance of perspective. A distorted perspective is rather typical of all legalistic religions because they concentrate on codes of conduct and easily become superficial. First-century Pharisees are by no means the only ones who have sometimes lost all sense of proportion. It can still happen, and does happen, and most of us are vulnerable at one time or another. So often it is the little things—little things magnified all out of proportion—that separate people. Perhaps it is only a questionable inflection of the voice, a misunderstood word, a word poorly chosen, an unintended slight, or a forgotten courtesy; and suddenly a wedge is driven between friends. Simple misunderstandings have a way of growing beyond repair, until people who need each other turn their backs on each other. Congregations seldom are disturbed by big issues. More often trifles get trumpeted, transformed, and magnified into big problems.

Jesus attempted to restore perspective to those so critical of Him by appealing to their own tradition. Straightforwardly He said, "Which of you, having a son or an ox that has fallen into a well, will not immediately pull him out on a sabbath day?" (14:5).

A footnote in the Revised Standard Version points

out that "other ancient authorities read *an ass*" instead of "a son": "Which of you having an ass or an ox that has fallen into a well. . . ." Should this reading be permitted, the argument is basically the same: mercy takes precedence over sabbath law, and mercy should not be limited to self-interest.

The reply to Jesus was silence. To respond would be to admit the validity of His critique of their piety. Their tradition did give precedence to mercy. To admit this would be to forfeit their right to criticize Him; and so compelling was their desire to criticize that their silence parallels the idea behind a colloquial expression sometimes used today: "My mind's made up; don't confuse me with facts!"

II

Jesus now takes command of the table conversation. If their defense of the distorted importance of sabbath-keeping is silence, then will they remain silent when other popular pieties are challenged?

The second piety questioned was the easy assumption that Pharisees were superior—religiously—to everyone else. Jesus used an illustration that sounded like ordinary folk-wisdom concerning the virtues of humility. Don't take places of honor at a marriage feast, He said, lest a more prominent guest arrive and you be asked to leave the place of honor and sit elsewhere. It appears, however, that Luke believed Jesus was doing more than repeating proverbial wisdom about social graces. Luke calls this illustration a parable, which immediatey invests it with a dimension of religious truth far beyond the concerns of etiquette. Jesus was puncturing popular piety by saying to the Pharisees that pushing for places of honor at the table placed them in grave danger of humiliation. Their scramble for chief seats, their pride in being members of religion's most exclusive club, their drive to be recognized as superior to everyone else, was dangerous. Pride, and self-pronounced purity, separated them from others at the table. How could they be so sure they deserved the honors they claimed? What if God should say, "Give way to others"? Shame would then force them to take lower places. Unfortunately, Pharisees simply could not imagine such a reversal. God's approval was assumed, taken for granted. How could God fail to approve? Were they not better? Were they not more worthy of approval than all the careless, unwashed sinners?

The second illustration, or parable, was addressed to His host, but clearly Jesus intended the word for all. This barb was directed against religion when it becomes a mutual admiration and mutual benefit society. When you entertain, don't just invite kith and kin, rich neighbors and close friends, lest, said Jesus, they also invite you in return and you be repaid. Invite those who cannot repay—the poor, the maimed, the lame, the blind. "You will be repaid at the resurrection of the just" (v. 14).

Once again Jesus was expressing a dimension of religious truth far beyond the concerns of etiquette, or how to care for the less fortunate. Pharisees, like adherents of popular pieties in other generations,

49

followed the natural human desire to associate with those like themselves. They exalted this desire into a religious principal. It became a standard of piety to refuse contact with those less devout. It became a symbol of holiness not to break bread with all lesser breeds outside the law!

The chumminess of like-minded zealots may be pleasant and mutually supportive, but those who only reflect one another's virtues miss the exalted blessedness of those who live with kindness and helpfulness to others with never a thought of reward.

Jesus might just as well have spoken into the air with none to hear. One of the guests blurted out the pious platitude, "Blessed is he who shall eat bread in the kingdom of God" (v. 15).

It was popular, and it was pious, in Jesus' day to picture the kingdom of God as a great supper or banquet. So long as the concept was taken seriously, but not literally, it wasn't too bad an idea. It was something like the piety of a previous generation or two of our own who seemingly could not think of heaven except in terms of glittering gates of pearl and streets of gold. Anyway, it was popular then to picture the kingdom of God as a great banquet—the Messiah's banquet. The joy of the Messianic banquet was imbedded deeply in Jewish lore. Basically it was an expression of hope, the anticipation of rejoicing and of joy and of satisfaction and of fellowship with the Messiah and with all those who shall inherit the promises of God. But for this popular religious sentiment to be expressed just now, the very moment when their pieties were being challenged, sounds suspiciously like a defensive platitude that everyone would be expected to accept—even Jesus! Unfortunately, one implication is that no one would repeat this pious proverb without being quite convinced that he himself had a gilt-edged invitation in his hip pocket. He had already judged himself worthy of God's great banquet, and every time he fasted and prayed and tithed and went to the synagogue, he was reaching into his pocket to touch that invitation!

III

Despite this platitude, Jesus continued in command of the table talk. It is as though He said to this pious gentleman and all those present, "Look, you are right! You do have an invitation to God's banquet, but you are making light of it. You seem to think this kingdom banquet is off somewhere in the future. On that point you are wrong! The time for the banquet is now. Your immediate response is demanded. I am saying to you now, 'Come, for all is now ready!' In rejecting me, you are rejecting the kingdom. In rejecting me, you reject God's gracious invitation, and you are doing it in a way that is not only silly but actually insulting."

Kenneth Bailey, professor of New Testament at the University of Beirut and for twenty years a careful student of village life and customs in the Near East, does a perfectly delightful cassette-tape commentary on this parable of the great banquet as illuminated by village customs still to be observed in the Near East. Dr. Bailey makes it quite clear that the so-called excuses for not attending the feast after having accepted the invitation were not just humorous excuses but calculated insults.

The great word for us to hear—just as it was the important word for the Pharisees to hear—is that the banquet is not canceled, even if the religiously elite and the privileged do not respond. Likewise, no one is excluded from God's kingdom except by his own choice.

At that time, popular piety assumed that only the righteous could ever sit at God's table. The gospel that Jesus came preaching was destructive of such status-seeking piety because He spoke of God's love for all men. He spoke of a God who rejoices over every sinner who repents, who seeks even one lost sheep, who waits like a watchful father for a rebellious son to return home, and then holds back nothing from the son who worked at home or the son who wasted his substance.

If the righteous are angry with God for being so good to sinners, and if, like the older brother, they refuse to participate in the feasting and the joy, then they shut themselves out of the kingdom.

IV

It would not be difficult to list a few popular pieties that need puncturing today. Every generation has its pet pieties, and we are not exceptions. Rather than listing such a series, and then popping them like balloons on a dart board just for the fun of hearing the noise, should we not be concerned to hear the gospel in this table talk? After all, it is the gospel, not our cleverness, that punctures every false piety. And the good news of the gospel is that God is more generous and more gracious than we can even think or imagine.

If we search to find ourselves in our Lord's parable, then consider the possibility that we are the ones far away, those wandering the world's highways, sleeping behind stone hedges! God's servants found us with an invitation that seems too good to be true. We are invited to God's banquet table, not because of our wealth or position, not because of our prestige or knowledge, not because of our attainments or piety, for we are the poor, the maimed, the lame, and the blind!

If we do not respond, if we do not accept, if we will not enter, then God calls those who will. No one's stubbornness is permitted to ruin his celebration. His house will be filled.

Through the Cross and through the Resurrection, and by the gift of the Holy Spirit at Pentecost, the kingdom of God has been thrown open to all believers. But now, as always, an invitation must be accepted. The gospel is the good news of God's redeeming love; but good news must be heard, and love must be accepted. Amen.

VI. Evangelism Is . . .

Scripture: He entered Jericho and was passing through. And there was a man named Zacchaeus; he was a chief tax collector, and rich. And he sought to see who Jesus was, but could not, on account of the crowd, because he was small of stature. So he ran on ahead and climbed up into a sycamore tree to see him, for he was to pass that way. And when Jesus came to the place, he looked up and said to him, "Zacchaeus, make haste and come down; for I must stay at your house today."

So he made haste and came down, and received him joyfully. And when they saw it they all murmured, "He has gone in to be the guest of a man who is a sinner."

And Zacchaeus stood and said to the Lord, "Behold, Lord, the half of my goods I give to the poor; and if I have defrauded anyone of anything, I restore it fourfold. And Jesus said to him, "Today salvation has come to this house, since he also is a son of Abraham. For the Son of man came to seek and to save the lost." (Luke 19:1-10)

I

In the story of Zacchaeus, Jesus invited Himself to dinner: "Zacchaeus, make haste and come down; for I must stay at your house today" (v. 5).

Luke calls Zacchaeus a "chief tax collector," which

may mean he had purchased the taxation rights for Jericho from the Roman government and that other tax collectors worked for him on a commission basis. In any case, Zacchaeus is both rich and despised. He is despised for stooping so low as to collect taxes from fellow Jews for the Roman government. He is further despised for luring others into such a hated occupation. Riches bring him contemptuous disdain because ill-gotten.

Zacchaeus climbed up into a sycamore tree to get a good view of Jesus. "He was small of stature," says Luke. There is also the possibility that it was not wise for Zacchaeus to mix with crowds on city streets. Why risk ridicule or even violence? Once Jesus calls attention to the presence of Zacchaeus up that sycamore tree, do you suppose it possible that His inviting Himself to go to his house that day was a way of safely escorting Zacchaeus home? Crowds have been known to be emotional and excitable, and one taunt, one howl of delight at seeing a rich enemy defenselessly caught up a tree, might have been enough to excite angry actions of hostility and vengeance. In any case, Luke reports that Zacchaeus "made haste and came down, and received him joyfully" (v. 6). If this interpretation is possible and permissible, then Zacchaeus' curiosity about Jesus had gotten him into a precarious position, and the apparent forwardness of the invitation to dinner was his rescue. It is possible. Luke does report that the crowd, "when they saw it . . . all murmured, 'He has gone in to be the guest of a man who is a sinner' "

(v. 7). The story is told with such picturesque detail as to make Zacchaeus unforgettable.

II

The setting is that Jesus had made up His mind to go to Jerusalem. "Taking the twelve, he said to them, 'Behold, we are going up to Jerusalem, and everything that is written of the Son of man by the prophets will be accomplished. For he will be delivered to the Gentiles, and will be mocked and shamefully treated and spit upon; they will scourge him and kill him, and on the third day he will rise.' But they understood none of these things; . . . they did not grasp what was said" (18:31-34).

Jericho was a stopover city on the way to Jerusalem. It was not so large as Jerusalem, but it was an important and wealthy city, nestled in the Jordan valley, commanding the crossings of the Jordan River and the approach to Jerusalem. For generations it had been famous for its great palm trees, and the dates grown there, and balsam groves. So beautiful and pleasant was Jericho that some spoke of it as an Eden. Jericho was both busy and rich—busy with priests from Jerusalem and with pilgrims on their way to the many festivals in the holy city, and rich from its natural products and the lucrative tourist trade.

We hazard the guess, however, that Jericho was no Eden for Zacchaeus. Jericho may have made him rich, but could it make him happy? People imagine sometimes that happiness will not matter if wealth is great enough. In real life this fantasy seldom holds true. To be estranged from our fellows, to deny our religion and our heritage, to feel separated from God, are losses money does not replace. When we lose the respect of others, we lose self-respect; and when self-respect is lost, so are dignity and inner peace.

Of Zacchaeus we read, "He sought to see Jesus." Why? Was it curiosity? Had he heard stories of this nonconformist rabbi who "receives sinners and eats with them"? Was it loneliness? Was it his conscience? Had he heard the story of Levi, now Matthew, once a tax collector like himself, but now a follower of this new teacher? Who can say? Perhaps it was only curiosity, and such is the mystery of personality that Zacchaeus, despite all he possessed, was eager to see what Jesus looked like. The English translation is awkward: it reads, "And he sought to see who Jesus was. . . " "To see who Jesus was": is this more than just seeing him? Anyway, because of the crowds he cannot see, so he runs ahead, climbs up into a tree, "to see him, for he was to pass that way" (v. 4). Let none speak lightly of curiosity! Curiosity can be the beginning of salvation, especially for those curious enough to want to see.

III

The conversation that day is where the action is. The words spoken are all important.

There may be significance in the fact that Zacchaeus stands when he speaks to Jesus. Presumably Jesus, Zacchaeus, and the disciples all have now entered the house. The meal has been prepared and served, or possibly they are eating now. Luke writes, "And Zacchaeus *stood* and said to the Lord . . ." (v. 8). Does any commentary see significance in this action? Do Bible students even mention it? In Western culture, standing has significance as a way of showing honor and respect. But this may not have been true at all in the culture of the Middle East. Oriental culture generally considers kneeling or bowing to the ground a more customary gesture of honor. Is it possible that any scandalously rich man impulsive enough to run, and then climb a tree, would also be impulsive enough to interrupt the meal, springing up from the low couch upon which he reclined, to declare, "Behold, Lord, the half of my goods I give to the poor." Rich men seldom make such rash statements—except for some profound, life-changing experience. When conversion includes the pocketbook and the bank account it becomes believable!

Bible commentaries say that Zacchaeus outdoes all legal requirements with his offer of fourfold restitution. More important than legal concepts of restitution is what this story says to us about evangelism and conversion. I remember the witness of a man who expressed appreciation for all his church meant to himself, his family, and especially to two teen-agers in his family. With deep feeling, he said he thanked God for church-school teachers, sponsors, and the many caring and loving adults who made his teen-agers feel so at home in their church. Then, speaking of his son, he said, "He's a person who needs someone to look up to." That expression stuck. Is there any one of us who doesn't need someone to look up to? That phrase could apply to Zacchaeus, and to a definition of what evangelism is all about.

First let's flip the phrase: Jesus looked at Zacchaeus. He looked up and said to him, "Zacchaeus, come down." Now, did Luke intend us to see significance in this rich man's name? Is it irony? The name "Zacchaeus" means "pure, righteous." Zacchaeus was anything but righteous and pure. Perhaps he wasn't bad in the sense of being so immoral, but he confesses himself a defrauder, and his enemies considered him a betrayer of his country and a destroyer of their faith. Yet, a wonderful change came for Zacchaeus because Jesus looked up to him and called him by name and accepted him. That is evangelism. Conversion began for Zacchaeus with acceptance.

Flip the phrase again and say that conversion continued when Zacchaeus began to look up to Jesus! "Zacchaeus stood and said . . . , 'Behold, Lord. . . .' Jesus said to him, 'Today salvation has come to this house, since he also is a son of Abraham' " (vv. 8, 9).

There are people today who feel turned off by the churches and by preachers and by Christian lifestyles they consider outdated. Many, we fear, are missing all opportunities for the life-transforming experiences they really seek because they will not give the church, or the Christian gospel, a chance. The best evangelism is not to say to them, "Brother, are you saved?" Why not ask: "Are you a person who needs to look up to someone? Whom do you look up to? If you don't look up to Jesus, is it because you don't know enough about Him? And if you would like to

59

know more, there is more we both can learn together. Don't reject Him until you know Him."

This is what Christians are: Christians are people who look up to Jesus. I'm aware, naturally, that Christian commitment is more than hero worship, but I have questions about theologies so sophisticated, and church education so therapeutically inspired and self-help oriented, that the name of Jesus is seldom mentioned. Make no mistake: if it were not for Jesus there would be no theologies, no Christian movement, and no Christian churches at all. These exist only because there was something in Jesus that made others look up to Him. We talk rather learnedly sometimes about finding God in Christ. More often the truth is the other way around: in Jesus, God finds us and claims us.

IV

Luke concludes the dramatic story of Zacchaeus by affirming that this is when Jesus said, "For the Son of man came to seek and to save the lost." Seeking and saving the lost—yes, how true! Jesus was always doing this, wasn't He? Peter, Mary Magdelene, Matthew, the lad with convulsions, the man possessed whose name was "legion"—all these sick, helpless, hopeless, misplaced people—sought and saved by Jesus. And now Zacchaeus. And I think Luke wants us to see that what happened to Zacchaeus in Jericho was just a "little symbol" of what will happen in Jerusalem, and later, in all the world. Even on the day of His death in Jerusalem, two others were crucified too. But one of them looked up to Jesus and said, "Remember me when you come into your kingdom" (Luke 23:42).

Sometimes Christians have been careless in their use of the word "lost." So far as I can tell, the New Testament does not use the word in the sense of doomed or damned. It simply means "in the wrong place." Remember the great fifteenth chapter of Luke: it is all about the "lost"—a lost coin, a lost sheep, and two lost sons. A coin may be lost through someone's carelessness. A sheep may be lost through a shepherd's oversight. It just wandered away. Sons may be lost willfully, by their own decisions, either at home or away. To save is to find, to restore, to bring back to its rightful place.

Today can be the day of salvation for any one of us, the day when we are recognized for what we are: sons of Abraham, men and women who "look to Jesus," the author and finisher of our faith. Amen.

VII. Sad and Sacred

Scripture: And when the hour came, he sat at table, and the apostles with him. And he said to them, "I have earnestly desired to eat this passover with you before I suffer; for I tell you I shall not eat it until it is fulfilled in the kingdom of God." And he took a cup, and when he had given thanks he said, "Take this, and divide it among yourselves; for I tell you that from now on I shall not drink of the fruit of the vine until the kingdom of God comes." And he took bread, and when he had given thanks he broke it and gave it to them, saying, "This is my body which is given for you. Do this in remembrance of me." And likewise the cup after supper, saying, "This cup which is poured out for you is the new covenant in my blood. But behold the hand of him who betrays me is with me on the table. For the Son of man goes as it has been determined; but woe to that man by whom he is betrayed!" And they began to question one another, which of them it was that would do this.

A dispute also arose among them, which of them was to be regarded as the greatest. And he said to them, "The kings of the Gentiles exercise lordship over them; and those in authority over them are called benefactors. But not so with you; rather let the greatest among you become as the youngest, and the leader as one who serves. For which is the greater, one who sits at table, or one who serves? Is it not the one who sits at table? But I am among you as one who serves.

"You are those who have continued with me in my trials; and I assign to you, as my Father assigned to me, a kingdom, that you may eat and drink at my table in my kingdom, and sit on thrones judging the twelve tribes of Israel.

"Simon, Simon, behold, Satan demanded to have you, that he might sift you like wheat, but I have prayed for you that your faith may not fail; and when you have turned again, strengthen your brethren." And he said to him, "Lord, I am ready to go with you to prison and to death." He said, "I tell you, Peter, the cock will not crow this day, until you three times deny that you know me."

And he said to them, "When I sent you out with no purse or bag or sandals, did you lack anything?" They said, "Nothing." He said to them, "But now, let him who has a purse take it, and likewise a bag. And let him who has no sword sell his mantle and buy one. For I tell you that this scripture must be fulfilled in me, 'And he was reckoned with transgressors'; for what is written about me has its fulfillment." And they said, "Look, Lord, here are two swords." And he said to them, "It is enough." (Luke 22:14-38)

I

Luke was impressed that Jesus broke bread with all sorts of people, disregarding all table fellowship taboos so carefully observed by the orthodox religious. In his short Gospel (only thirty-six pages in the version quoted here), Luke tells of six different occasions when Jesus sat at table with others. Each time he also reports on the conversations that took place. In this seventh meal everything is reversed: Jesus is host, not guest. The conversation is not with Pharisees, scribes, or Sadducees, nor with people who have wandered in from the streets. This meal is

for and with the Twelve. Jesus had no home of His
own in which to entertain disciples, so use was made
of the home of friends. Some think the friends none
other than the parents of the young John Mark. All we
know is that the house where the meal took place was
in Jerusalem, and that it contained "a large upper
room, furnished"—also called "the guest room."

To read carefully Luke's account of what has come
to be known as the Last Supper, and of the
conversations taking place during that meal, causes
two words to come to mind: sacred and sad. Such a
sacred scene it was, and, at the same time, so sad. Is it
often true, or is it incidental, that the sad and the
sacred nudge so close to each other, like laughter and
tears, or love and hate?

II

"When the hour came" Jesus took His place at the
table. The apostles were with Him. Luke takes care to
call them apostles. In his mind, he already sees these
men as representatives of the church that is to be.

Jesus began the conversation by giving His apostles
a glimpse into His mind and heart. He had "earnestly
desired to eat this passover" with them, He said,
before suffering. Time was running out. This was
Thursday evening. It is entirely possible that the only
morsel of food to pass His lips between now and His
death on Friday afternoon will be this sip of wine, and
bread torn from the loaf.

The bond of unity between Jesus and apostles
symbolized by that shared cup and the loaf broken

and passed among them was marred by the presence of the betrayer—Judas, the enigma of that day and hour, and the enigma of the centuries. "Behold the hand of him who betrays me is with me on the table." Jesus expressed no sadness for Himself as the one betrayed, only for the betrayer: "Woe to that man by whom he is betrayed!" How much can love endure? The betrayer was there, seated at the table with them, but not identified. "They began to question one another, which of them it was that would do this."

After supper two topics of conversation predominated. First a dispute among them as to who should rank highest and be regarded as greatest. Without obvious reprimand, Jesus insisted that a new standard must prevail among them: service is to be the way to greatness. Then, recognizing that these men have continued with Him faithfully, despite opposition and disappointments, Jesus spoke of the rule they would bear one day in the church. To eat and drink at His table in His kingdom, and to judge the twelve tribes of Israel, was again a symbolic way of speaking of the church as the new Israel, with twelve apostles as deliberate representatives of the twelve tribes.

No sooner was praise spoken, and honors promised, than a warning was also issued. Students are aware that the words addressed to Simon are not as straightforward as they appear in English. "Simon, Simon, behold, Satan demanded to have you"; and the Greek word here for "you" is plural. "But I have prayed for you," and here the word is singular, "that your faith may not fail; and when you have turned again, strengthen your brethren" (v. 32). It is as though Jesus had said, "Satan has already taken one of you, and would capture all of you, if he could—including you, Simon!" Then Simon, so falsely sure of himself, so confident that neither prison nor death could ever lead him astray, heard the dismaying prediction that the night would not end before he denied his Lord, not once, but three times! How ominous this whole conversation became, with disturbing, tragic words being spoken, words like "betray," "deny," "sift like wheat."

Yes, soon everything is to be so different. Do they remember those pleasant days in Galilee when He commissioned seventy of them to go before Him and prepare His way? Without purse or bag or sandals they had gone and had lacked nothing. They returned with such excitement and joy saying, "Lord, even the demons are subject to us in your name" (10:17). That day, said Jesus, is done and over and gone. "This scripture must be fulfilled in me, 'And he was reckoned with transgressors' " (22:37). As His followers, they will be known as accomplices of a transgressor. The back of every man's hand will be against them. If they have purse or bag, take them. If they have no sword, then sell their mantle and buy one! Did Jesus mean this literally? Of course not! Sometimes Jesus used the violent metaphor, the exaggerated figure of speech, to make a point emphatic. Several such expressions can be identified, such as "If your right eye causes you to sin, pluck it out and throw it away. . . . If your right hand causes you to sin, cut it off . . ." (Matt. 5:29, 30); "It is easier for a camel to go through the eye of a needle than for a rich man to enter the kingdom of God" (Mark 10:25); "You blind guides, straining out a gnat and swallowing a camel!" (Matt. 23:24). This metaphor also was misunderstood. Missing the meaning entirely, the disciples say, "Look, Lord, here are two swords." "It is enough," said Jesus. Today we would put His reply as slang and say, "Forget it! If you don't understand, don't ask me to explain." Yet, believe it or not, Pope Boniface VIII, in his bull *Unam Sanctam,* based the doctrine that God has entrusted to the church two swords—meaning both spiritual and civil authority—on this verse. Thus was the sword baptized as religious authority! History suggests that power can be as demonic when the Church becomes the State as when the State becomes the Church.

III

This meal scene in an upper room, and the sad and sacred words spoken there—what do they mean to us today?

First, it helps to understand that meal when seen in the context of the Passover. Those who sat with Jesus at that table would have so understood it. The basic idea of the Passover was emancipation, deliverance from the slavery and bondage of Egypt, safety through the blood of the Pasover Lamb which had been smeared on the doorpost of the houses of the children of Israel when the angel of death slew the firstborn of the Egyptians (Exodus 12). Jesus was, therefore, explaining Himself to His disciples in terms of

67

emancipation, liberation, redemption, freedom—not from Egypt, for that slavery was past—but liberation from sin and death and hell. Furthermore, all the intentions of God were behind their redemption through His sacrifice. As He said, "For the Son of man goes as it has been determined" (v. 22).

Second, it helps to understand that meal when seen in the context of the covenant. Israel firmly believed that God had established a covenant with them. They were to be His people; He was to be their God. The laws of God bound them to one another. By obeying His laws, the people were obedient to God. In breaking His laws the people were disobedient to God, rejecting the covenant. The fundamental truth behind this concept is that one great function of religion is to give people access to God. As the psalmist lamented, "When shall I come and behold the face of God?" (Psalm 42:2b). Israel believed that access to God came by keeping His laws. Their tragedy was that sin kept blocking that access. Sin kept putting barriers between God and His people. The whole sacrificial system of the Jews had as its one aim and object the restoration of the relationship between God and man which sin kept destroying. The priests, whose function was to stand between God and His people, interpreting the laws of God to the people and interceding for, and making sacrifices in behalf of, the sins of the people, were, unfortunately, sinful men themselves. They had to offer sacrifices for their own sins before offering sacrifices for the sins of the people. What was needed, as is said so pointedly in the New Testament Epistle to the Hebrews, was a perfect priest and a perfect sacrifice, both of which were fulfilled in Jesus. What Luke is saying, as do the other accounts of the Last Supper, is that by His life and death, at the cost of His body and blood, Jesus established a new covenant with God, based not on a relationship of law but on a relationship of redemptive love.

Prophets of the Old Testament sometimes used a special way of getting their messages across. If people would not listen, they might dramatize their message by some attention-getting or sensational action. We call this "prophetic dramatic action." Jeremiah, for instance, when people would not listen as he spoke of their being enslaved by Nebuchadnezzar, put a yoke and a bar about his neck and the thongs of a slave on his feet (Jeremiah 27). At one time Isaiah went about for three years stripped and barefoot to warn of the threat of captivity by the Assyrians. Hosea gave symbolic names to his sons and daughters, making them walking witnesses to his messages. Isaiah did the same with his two sons. The story of one son, especially, provokes sympathy, for he was named *Mahershalalhashbaz*—"the spoil speedeth; the prey hasteth" (Isa. 8:3, 4). The first son's name wasn't quite so bad: *Shearjashub*—meaning "a remnant shall return" (Isa. 7:3).

Jesus also used dramatic prophetic action. This, many believe, is the meaning of the so-called triumphal entry into Jerusalem. He rode an animal of peace. When kings came in peace, they rode asses. When riding to war, they rode horses. The cleansing of the temple was another dramatic prophetic action.

Now, here in the Upper Room, is another. "Look," He was saying, "look at this red wine poured into a cup. My red blood shall also be poured out—for you! And just as I break this bread, so my body will be broken—and it will be for you. They will do this to me, but all that happens to me is for your sakes." In this manner Jesus was walking in the tradition of the prophets, making others see and understand by actions what words alone could never fully tell.

IV

In the great good providence of God, triumph was on the other side of tragedy. Resurrection followed Crucifixion; and thus that which was both sad and sacred has been transformed for us into the joyful feast of the people of God, when men and women come from the east and the west, and from the north and the south, and sit at table in the kingdom of God, celebrating the sacrament that proclaims the gospel of God's love, a love that triumphs over every foe in the kingdom that is, and that is to be. Amen.

VIII. The Guest Who Surprises

Scripture: That very day two of them were going to a village named Emmaus, about seven miles from Jerusalem, and talking with each other about all these things that had happened. While they were talking and discussing together, Jesus himself drew near and went with them. But their eyes were kept from recognizing him. And he said to them, "What is this conversation which you are holding with each other as you walk?" And they stood still, looking sad. Then one of them, named Cleopas, answered him, "Are you the only visitor to Jerusalem who does not know the things that have happened there in these days?" And he said to them, "What things?" And they said to him, "Concerning Jesus of Nazareth, who was a prophet mighty in deed and word before God and all the people, and how our chief priests and rulers delivered him up to be condemned to death, and crucified him. But we had hoped that he was the one to redeem Israel. Yes, and besides all this, it is now the third day since this happened. Moreover, some women of our company amazed us. They were at the tomb early in the morning and did not find his body; and they came back saying that they had even seen a vision of angels, who said that he was alive. Some of those who were with us went to the tomb, and found it just as the women had said; but him they did not see." And he said to them, "O foolish men, and slow of heart to believe all that the prophets have spoken! Was it not necessary that the Christ should suffer these

71

things and enter into his glory?" And beginning with Moses and all the prophets, he interpreted to them in all the scriptures the things concerning himself.

So they drew near to the village to which they were going. He appeared to be going further, but they constrained him, saying, "Stay with us, for it is toward evening and the day is now far spent." So he went in to stay with them. When he was at table with them, he took the bread and blessed, and broke it, and gave it to them. And their eyes were opened and they recognized him; and he vanished out of their sight. They said to each other, "Did not our hearts burn within us while he talked to us on the road, while he opened to us the scriptures?" And they rose that same hour and returned to Jerusalem; and they found the eleven gathered together and those who were with them, who said, "The Lord has risen indeed, and has appeared to Simon!" Then they told what had happened on the road, and how he was known to them in the breaking of the bread. (Luke 24:13-35)

I

When Luke wrote his Gospel, the Jewish people were very exclusive as far as table fellowship with Gentiles was concerned. Being a Gentile himself, and having experienced the hurts of exclusion, Luke must have loved Jesus all the more for the open, accepting way in which He sat at table and ate and drank with those considered unworthy and unclean by religious people. Luke also reports the persistent charge brought against Jesus by Scribes and Pharisees: "This man receives sinners and eats with them" (15:2). Luke—and Luke alone—makes it quite clear that Jesus knew His table fellowship with sinners was a scandal to His own people. He reports that Jesus reminded His people that because John the Baptist neither ate bread nor drank wine it was said of him that he was demon-possessed. He, in turn, not being an ascetic, but eating the bread and drinking the wine of those who entertained Him, was accused of being a glutton and a drunkard (7:14).

Because of Luke's special interest in the table talk and the meal scenes involving Jesus, he reports no less than six meal scenes in his short Gospel. The seventh meal was altogether different because Jesus was host, not guest. The conversation was not with Scribes, Pharisees, or people who wandered in from the streets, but was a private dinner in a special room in a private home. Jesus planned that meal because He earnestly desired to eat the Passover with the Twelve before the suffering that was to come to Him (cf. 22:15). That sad but sacred meal has been transformed for us into the joyful feast of the people of God.

II

Palm Sunday focuses attention on the triumphal entry into Jerusalem, and the documented events of the last week of Jesus' life. Let's explore the relationships and associations between the Thursday evening dinner in that Upper Room in the holy city and the Sunday evening dinner in the little village of Emmaus. In time and space those two dinners were separated by only three days and seven miles, but those two dinners, and the events that occurred between them, have changed the world—and all of life, for all of us.

73

For the stimulation of it, think of the similarities and differences in those two dinners.

The Upper Room dinner was a religious festival. It was a Passover celebration. Jesus used that occasion to tell His disciples something about Himself. All the intention of God for the deliverance of mankind from bondage to sin, death, and hell were behind his sacrifice. "The Son of man goes as it has been determined," He said. At the cost of His life, Jesus was opening up a new access to God, establishing a new Covenant with God, reconciling the world to God.

The dinner at Emmaus was not a religious festival, just an ordinary meal. Yet the surprising Guest at that humble table transformed their simple meal into one of great religious significance because the resurrected, redeemed, transformed, and glorified Jesus was recognized by them as Guest and Host and Lord. Was this Luke's way of saying that no meal is ever ordinary when the Guest who surprises is at the table?

The Thursday dinner was planned—carefully planned. The Sunday dinner appears almost accidental. Indications were that Jesus planned to continue His journey until the two, for whom Emmaus was their objective, said to Him, "Stay with us, for evening draws on, and the day is almost over" (Luke 24:28 NEB).

The Thursday dinner was for the Twelve: just Jesus and those He counted on the most, although one of them was a betrayer. Only three are at the Sunday evening dinner: Jesus, the surprising Guest who becomes Host, and two camp followers. Not only had these two known about Jesus, they had known Him.

74

Up to a point they were believers. "We had been hoping," they said, "that he [Jesus] was the man to liberate Israel" (24:21 NEB). In reporting the rumors of an empty tomb they also said, "Some women of *our company* have astounded us: they went early to the tomb, but failed to find his body, and returned with a story that they had seen a vision of angels who told them he was alive. So some of *our people* went to the tomb and found things just as the women had said; but him they did not see" (24:22-24 NEB. Italics mine). Apparently, then, they were camp followers of Jesus. They identified with Jesus and His people. Their dejection was that the hopes that had begun to build in them were now shattered.

Another contrast is that whereas the names of all the Twelve are known, even the name of in-famy—Judas Iscariot—there was one at that intimate table in Emmaus whose name is not known. Presumably his name was unknown to Luke. The identity of the two believers seems of small concern to Luke, for even the name of the one—Cleopas—is reported incidentally. Luke began his Emmaus story in simplest fashion, saying, "That very day two of them were going to a village named Emmaus." Later we learn that the "two" were not apostles—not two of the Twelve. Simple personal pronouns are used: "they" were talking with each other, or "we" had hoped. It is only after Jesus joins them, unrecognized, and asks what they are discussing, that Luke tells us that "one of them, named Cleopas, answered him, 'Are you the only visitor to Jerusalem who does not

75

know the things that have happened there in these days?' " (24:18).

Only this one time is this believer identified by name. That's not all: after this date he is never mentioned again. Only Luke tells this story, so his name does not appear in the other Gospels, nor in any Epistle, nor in any other place in all the New Testament.

Isn't it the strangest thing? Here is the most incredible event in all of history—the only miracle worthy of the name—the rejected, crucified Jesus is, by the power of God, raised from the dead, transformed, redeemed, glorified, given a new body of glory; and what happens? According to Luke, His first, or second, appearance is to a person unnamed and unknown, and to a man named Cleopas, who, after his witness to the Eleven, is never heard from again! So often, it seems, God lets the gospel hang by a thread, committing the future of his kingdom to insignificant people, unnamed and unknown. Or perhaps it is good that only one guest at the Emmaus table is named, because the one unnamed can represent any believer—all believers—because we are all unimportant until we have seen the Lord and have a message to tell.

There are other similarities and differences be-tween the Thursday dinner in Jerusalem and the Sunday evening dinner in Emmaus, but I mention only two more. One is the fact that neither Cleopas nor his companion participated in the Thursday dinner of religious celebration, yet when Jesus took bread and blessed and broke it and gave it to them at their table on Sunday evening, they recognized Him. The record says, "Their eyes were opened and they recognized him" (24:31).

Another contrast is the difference in mood and attitude between the two dinners. The setting, the symbolism, the conversation of the Upper Room keep bringing two words to the surface: sad and sacred. The impression is that the apostles rose from that table in painful silence. They followed Jesus to the garden of prayer; yet each went alone. They were together, yet each was surrounded by a sea of loneliness. "He [Jesus] came out, and went, as was his custom, to the Mount of Olives; and the disciples followed him" (22:39). In the garden, Luke says Jesus withdrew from them "about a stone's throw" (22:41), but who can measure the distance of loneliness? After that greatest of all prayers—"not my will, but thine, be done" (22:42)—Jesus returns to find them sleeping. "Why do you sleep? Rise and pray," He said, "that you may not enter into temptation" (22:46).

The two believers leave the Emmaus dinner with incredible news to share. On the road to Emmaus, Luke described them as having "faces full of gloom" (24:18 NEB). Three sad, tumultuous, tragic days in Jerusalem were enough to leave them emotionally exhausted. When hopes are shaken and shattered, weariness takes over. The gloom was gone from their faces now. If their meal began in weariness, it was forgotten now. "They rose that same hour and returned to Jerusalem" (24:33). Back to Jerusalem they go—seven miles away! As fast as they can they go, and by now it must be dark! And "they found the eleven gathered together and those who were with them." Where did they find them? Where were they gathered together? What were they doing? We don't know. Luke doesn't tell us. All we know is that before these two excited believers can speak, the apostles say, "The Lord has risen indeed, and has appeared to Simon!" (24:34). "Then they told what had happened on the road, and how he was known to them in the breaking of the bread" (24:35).

III

The earliest evidence for the Resurrection comes not from the Gospels, but from the Letters of Paul, particularly the fifteenth chapter of I Corinthians, believed to have been written at least ten years before Mark, the earliest Gospel account. Paul said he "delivered" to the Christians in Corinth "as of first importance" what he had also received, "that Christ died for our sins in accordance with the Scriptures, that he was buried, that he was raised on the third day in accordance with the scriptures, and that he appeared to Cephas, then to the twelve. Then he appeared to more than five hundred brethren at one time, most of whom are still alive, though some have fallen asleep" (I Cor. 15:3-6). Paul is quoted here because Luke supports his witness that Cephas —Peter—was among the first to see the risen Lord. Luke told of Peter's denial. He also wrote that when Jesus turned and looked at Peter, that big fisherman stumbled out of the courtyard of the high priest's house blinded with tears. "He . . . wept bitterly"

(22:62). Now it is as though the risen Lord was eager to tell Peter that all was forgiven. A penitent sinner's self-respect was restored! What a beautiful, sacred story.

We are grateful to Luke for underlining this tradition about Peter, and we are especialy grateful to the beloved Gentile physician for telling us the whole Emmaus story. It is his story. No one else tells it; and what a treasure it is! Luke doesn't describe the resurrection of Jesus—no evangelist does that—for no one can describe what God alone is capable of doing; but Luke reassures us that our Lord is known through the witness of the Scriptures, and the fellowship of broken bread and shared cup, and through the testimony of believers who share with one another what Jesus means to them. Amen.

IX. Too Good to Be True?

Scripture: As they were saying this, Jesus himself stood among them. But they were startled and frightened, and supposed that they saw a spirit. And he said to them, "Why are you troubled, and why do questionings rise in your hearts? See my hands and my feet, that it is I myself; handle me, and see; for a spirit has not flesh and bones as you see that I have." And while they still disbelieved for joy, and wondered, he said to them, "Have you anything here to eat?" They gave him a piece of broiled fish, and he took it and ate before them.

Then he said to them, "These are my words which I spoke to you, while I was still with you, that everything written about me in the law of Moses and the prophets and psalms must be fulfilled." Then he opened their minds to understand the scriptures, and said to them, "Thus it is written, that the Christ should suffer and on the third day rise from the dead, and that repentance and forgiveness of sins should be preached in his name to all nations, beginning from Jerusalem. You are witnesses of these things. And behold, I send the promise of my Father upon you; but stay in the city, until you are clothed with power from on high."

Then he led them out as far as Bethany, and lifting up his hands he blessed them. While he blessed them, he parted from them, and was carried up into heaven. And they returned to Jerusalem with great joy, and were continually in the temple blessing God. (Luke 24:36-53)

I

In his Gospel, Luke tells of three Resurrection appearances. The first was to Peter; the second was to the two at Emmaus; the third was to the Eleven, and others assembled with them, in Jerusalem. All these appearances take place on Sunday—the day of Resurrection.

The tradition of a first appearance to Peter suggests that the risen Lord was eager to let Peter know he was forgiven. On this same day, "the first day of the week," Jesus drew near and engaged in conversation with two gloomy believers on the road to Emmaus. Because it was "toward evening" and the day "far spent," the two invite Jesus to stay with them. Only when they were at table with Him did their surprising Guest become their Host. He "took the bread and blessed, and broke it, and gave it to them. And their eyes were opened and they recognized him" (24:32).

We have explored the similarities and differences, both in mood and attitude, between the Sunday evening meal in Emmaus and the Thursday evening dinner in Jerusalem with the Twelve. The two in Emmaus, their gloom and weariness forgotten, rose from the table with incredible news to share. "They rose that same hour and returned to Jerusalem" (v. 33). Back to Jerusalem they go—seven miles away! "They found the eleven gathered together and those who were with them" (v. 33). Before these excited, breathless believers can speak, the apostles say, "The Lord has risen indeed, and has appeared to Simon!"

(v. 34). "Then they told what had happened on the road, and how he was known to them in the breaking of the bread" (v. 35).

Our story begins at this very point: the Guest who surprises, surprises again. While the two from Emmaus were speaking, Jesus Himself stood among them. They thought they saw a spirit. They were startled and frightened. Jesus asked why they were troubled; then called attention to His hands and feet, saying, "It is I myself; handle me, and see" (v. 40).

This third appearance can also be considered a meal scene. Consider this incredible sentence: "And while they still disbelieved for joy, and wondered, he said to them, 'Have you anything here to eat?' They gave him a piece of broiled fish, and he took it and ate before them" (vv. 41-43).

In his history of the early church, when Luke summarizes Peter's sermon in the home of Cornelius, the Roman Centurian, he reports the sermon as a rehearsal of the basic elements of the Christian story, quoting Peter as saying, "We are witnesses to all that [Jesus] did both in the country of the Jews and in Jerusalem. They put him to death by hanging him on a tree; but God raised him on the third day and made him manifest; not to all the people but to us who were chosen by God as witnesses, who ate and drank with him after he rose from the dead" (Acts 10:39-41). Apparently, then, a tradition of eating and drinking with Jesus after the Resurrection was one basic element of the kerygma—the common proclamation of the Christian community.

II

Our first response to Luke's story of Jesus' third appearance on Easter Sunday is to ask, What can we make of all this? Because of our basic orientation to Greek habits of thought, such as a duality of body and soul, a preference for universal truths and for abstract thought, and a persistent desire to "spiritualize" the material, our reaction is: What can *intelligent* people make of all this? Was it necessary for Luke to be so specific? Why was it important to him that the redeemed, transformed, and glorified Jesus should say, "Have you anything here to eat?" Why was it essential to add that Jesus took the broiled fish "and ate before them"?

It was much less difficult to talk about the Sunday evening dinner in Emmaus because a eucharistic significance can always be seen in the phrases about taking bread and breaking it and blessing it and giving it to them. Further, the statement that "their eyes were opened and they recognized him" (24:31) can always be interpreted as sudden insight or spiritual perception. Later, perhaps while trying to explain their own failure to recognize Him earlier, the Emmaus believers were not satisfied to speak only of their dullness or of their "slowness of heart to believe," or of their superficial knowledge of scripture. They could only assume that some supernatural restraint had been imposed upon their vision, a restraint not removed until Jesus broke bread before them.

As previously stated, Luke does not describe the resurrection of Jesus. No evangelist does that, because

83

no one can describe what God alone can do. At the same time, Luke does want to be sure we take seriously the reality of the Resurrection. To say that Jesus ate before them was another way of saying that this really was Jesus who came and stood among the disciples. This was Jesus—no ghost, no apparition. This was the same Jesus who shared the Passover with them in the Upper Room on the Thursday before his death. Jesus was real—real but different. He was in bodily form, yet changed so as not to be subject to all ordinary physical restrictions.

The subject of my dissertation for my master of theology degree was "The New Testament Doctrine of the Resurrection of the Body," so I have at least been exposed to some of the dimensions of this problem of the nature of the Resurrection body. That project was an in-depth study involving several years' time, the reading of hundreds of books, the writing and rewriting of several hundred pages of agonized composition; but it was a challenge I shall always be grateful I attempted. That study left me with a deposit of a half-dozen words that still come to mind whenever attempting to think or speak of the mystery of the Resurrection body—words such as changed, transformed, redeemed, glorified, a body of glory, change but continuity, renewed and transformed but identifiable.

That study also made me aware of the essential differences between the Greek attitude toward the body as the prison-house of the soul, and the Hebrew, or biblical, attitude of the unity of body and soul. The Bible understands humanity by looking at us in relationship to God. We are living beings only because God created us in his own image and breathed into our nostrils the breath of life. The Bible does not think of anything in humanity, however noble, that is not subject to death. Nothing about humanity is "by nature" incorruptible. "All flesh is grass, and all its beauty is like the flower of the field" (Isa. 40:6). The first lie recorded in Scripture is when man listened to the creature instead of the Creator, and believed it when he was told, "You will not die" (Gen. 3:4). Christianity can only understand "resurrection" when it is God's action, and it can only understand the resurrection body as God's gift. "God gives it a body as he has chosen, and to each kind of seed its own body" (I Cor. 15:38). "The wages of sin is death, but the free gift of God is eternal life in Christ Jesus our Lord" (Rom. 6:23).

III

Because I have been bold enough to refer to an in-depth study I once made on the Resurrection, I should want no one to assume either that I consider myself an authority with wisdom above others, or that I am beyond the point of ever struggling with doubt myself. Both would be untrue.

I have great respect for Dr. William Barclay, for twenty-seven years a member of the divinity faculty of the University of Glasgow, and a great New Testament scholar. I respect his biblical scholarship; I am excited by his teaching, and I loved him as a Christian disciple and as a man. He insisted he was not a theologian—though I thought him overmodest —but it interests me that he described himself as a "natural believer." He fled no debate, never ran from disagreement; but, says he, "In the deepest part of me there is a certainty which nothing can touch."

I wish I could always say the same of myself. Someday, perhaps. The phrase in Luke's description of the apostles in the presence of the risen Lord that grabbed me from the first time I read it is: "while they still disbelieved for joy, and wondered. . . ." Is the Resurrection too good to be true?

This attitude of wistfulness, of disbelieving for joy, of following hard to know the truth but always being suspicious of self-deception, of wanting to be a committed believer but insisting upon trying to understand our faith and being able to give a reason for the faith within, is a struggle that never quite ceases for some of us. The struggle is stronger at some times than others, of course, but it is a struggle that never quite ends. I still remember reaching a certain plateau in my dissertation—a time when I said to myself, in effect, that to push beyond a certain point in trying to "prove" the Resurrection or in trying to understand the miracle that God alone can perform, becomes an evidence not of faith but of the very opposite. To be alive, and to be human, is to experience the agonies of not knowing—not knowing what to do or where to go, of being yourself but never the self you ought to be and want to be. Nothing but an act of God can save us from the ache of the empty heart, or from the despair of an endless search for knowledge that never fully arrives, or from the reality of death as the final mockery of the highest of our human ideals and the most cherished of our human aspirations.

To confess that there are times and moments when we still "disbelieve for joy and wonder" is to say that the prayer many of us can identify with easiest is "Lord, I believe; help my unbelief!" (Mark 9:24). Not that we think the gospel too good to be true—not at all! It is too good not to be true. We cling, therefore, not to personal feelings of confidence, but to the conviction that Christ claims us. In spite of weakness and inconsistency—in spite of everything—we do believe Him when He said, "You did not choose me, but I chose you and appointed you that you should go and bear fruit" (John 15:16).

And just because of this wistfulness within us, we know how much we shall always need the church, the fellowship of believers. We need the church to say to us, "The Lord has risen indeed, and has appeared to Simon!" Thank God for Simon; and thank God for the church too. Thank God for every gathered congregation, and the hymns that are sung, and the faith and life that believers share with one another!

And just because of this wistfulness within, we know how much we need the Scriptures. I'm not being pious when I say that the more I study the Bible—read it, listen to it, search its beauty, and struggle with its problems—the more I read it, the more precious, the more wonderful and astonishing and important it becomes to me. Yes, and I thank God for Luke and his Gospel. I can understand why one New Testament scholar called it the most beautiful

book in the world. Luke's Gospel has a beauty, a
clarity, a charm of expression, and a holy restraint
about it that makes it so authentically beautiful, and a
joy forever.

Now and then I should say to myself: little man,
why should it be thought incredible with you if God
doth raise the dead? (Cf. Acts 26:8.)

X. Christian Worship

Scripture: Then he said to them, "These are my words which I spoke to you, while I was still with you, that everything written about me in the law of Moses and the prophets and the psalms must be fulfilled." Then he opened their minds to understand the scriptures, and said to them, "Thus it is written, that the Christ should suffer and on the third day rise from the dead, and that repentance and forgiveness of sins should be preached in his name to all nations, beginning from Jerusalem. You are witnesses of these things. And behold, I sent the promise of my Father upon you; but stay in the city, until you are clothed with power from on high." (Luke 24:44-53)

I

After making it clear that this Jesus who appeared to the disciples was not a ghost but the same Jesus who broke bread with them in the Upper Room on Thursday before His death, Luke makes it equally clear that a change has occurred. This is the same Jesus, but now in a body of glory—a changed, redeemed, transformed, glorified body—real, but not subject to the normal limitations of flesh and blood; changed, but still recognizable, transformed, but with an identifiable continuity. Luke also makes it clear that these appearances came to an end. This leave-taking is usually spoken of as the Ascension, but as Luke describes it here, there is no necessary implication that Jesus ascended vertically, stopping in a heaven a mile or so above the earth. In that beautifully restrained manner of his, Luke simply says that Jesus "parted from them" while He blessed them (24:51).

Just as there are sounds in the air we cannot hear until a radio pulls them in, and just as there are colors not to be seen by human eyes until captured by a television screen, so is it not possible to say that Jesus slipped into another order of existence not perceived by human senses? Luke made no effort to explain the Resurrection. There is no human way to explain an action God alone can perform. Likewise, I am not suggesting an explanation of the Ascension. It is enough to try to remove the mental handicap of thinking "up," or "vertical," when the word "ascension" need not be so circumscribed.

The emotional response of the disciples to the Ascension is what we should notice. Luke tells us "they returned to Jerusalem with great joy." Several ancient manuscripts add the phrase, "they worshiped him, and returned to Jerusalem with great joy." My persuasion is that the Revised Standard Version need not have placed the phrase about "worshiping Jesus" in a footnote. It harmonizes with Matthew's Gospel, which says plainly that when the disciples "saw him they worshiped him; but some doubted" (Matt. 28:17).

Luke began his Gospel in the temple in Jerusalem, telling of Zechariah and Elizabeth and the prophecy that their son, John the Baptist, was to prepare the way for Jesus, the Messiah. Now the circle is complete, for the disciples return to Jerusalem with great joy, and were "continually in the temple blessing God." They were back in the temple praising God, but now their worship of God was altogether different.

II

My concern is that we not slide over the profundity of that word "worship" when applied to Jesus. Whatever the disciples may have thought of Jesus during His ministry among them, there must be no sidestepping the fact that His passion, His resurrection, and His appearances to them, and now His final parting from them, made them feel it natural to worship Him while, at the same time, praising and blessing God in the temple. Up to this time they had freely spoken of Jesus as Master, Teacher, Prophet, even Lord. Now they worship Him as living Lord, adoring him in a way not possible before the Crucifixion and Resurrection. Looking into the face of Him whom God had raised from the dead, "they worshiped him."

The anticipation of this worship of the risen Lord is suggested in John's Gospel by the story of Thomas. Thomas said he could not believe the Resurrection, not unless he himself with his own eyes should see the risen Lord and touch the nail-scarred hands.

When Jesus again appeared to the disciples, and Thomas was with them, he fell to his knees, saying, "My Lord and my God!" (John 20:28).

The Resurrection was something so new and unexpected and stunning, and so good and wonderful, and so revolutionary, that the truth of it shattered old ways of thinking. It was a fact too big for words, bringing, as it did, such new joy, and such new knowledge and certainty of God, and such a new revelation of what God had done for them, that it commanded their worship of Him who was that revelation of God. No longer could they think of Jesus without thinking of what God had done for them through His life and death and resurrection. It took years of thinking and worshiping and wondering, before John the Beloved, at the end of a long life of discipleship, could say, "And the Word became flesh, and dwelt among us, full of grace and truth; we have beheld his glory, glory as of the only Son from the Father" (John 1:14).

III

Is it necessary—important—to stress this distinctive feature of Christian worship, namely, its Christ-centeredness? I believe it is. I seriously doubt, in fact, that the true nature, and the true genius, of Christian worship is understood at all until the Resurrection is taken seriously.

It was this Christ-centeredness of the worship of early Christians that so soon resulted in their exclusion from temple and synagogue. Having no places of their own for worship, they gathered in one another's homes or out of town beside a river, or on the rise of a hill at dawn. It was their faith in the Resurrection that brought them together on the first day of the week—Sunday, the day of Resurrection—assembling to sing and pray and rejoice and preach and teach and give their gifts of sacrificial love.

It is as true today as ever that the character of worship is shaped by our conception of God. As persons of the twentieth century living in a civilized country, our problem is not primitive idolatries or a worship prompted by fear. Neither is atheism our problem. Frankly, an honest, thoroughgoing atheism requires more credulity than most of us can muster! It requires more faith than we can put together to believe that human personality and intelligence and love and beauty and goodness are just meaningless accidents! The problem for contemporary man is not atheism but the vague, unreal, agnostic fuzziness that sets in whenever he tries to think of God. To worship an oblong blur, or an abstract idea, or a formula, is nonsense. This has been tried but no longer appeals. The day is gone when a synthetic god, conjured up by writing abstract terms in capital letters, can have any lasting appeal. To worship the "Great Mind" of the universe, or the "Great Spirit," or the "First Cause," or the "Prime Mover," or the "Principle of Concretion," or the "Ground of Being," or the "Great Oneness," or the "Principle of Truth" or "Love" or "Justice" is fuzziness itself compared to the sharp focus of worshiping God the Father Almighty, Maker of heaven and earth, and Jesus Christ, His only Son, our Lord, and the Holy Spirit, the Lord and Giver of life—one God, blessed forever!

It has always been difficult—granted, yes—for the church to explain how it can hold resolutely to monotheism—there is but one God—and yet to say that the glory of God is seen in the face of Jesus Christ, and that the Holy Spirit prompts us, quickens us, convicts us of sin, and leads us to respond to the love of God. Despite everything, the church keeps stammering out this confession, knowing full well that unless God *was* in Christ reconciling the world unto Himself, then worship is dull and trivial and meaningless. And without the work of the Holy Spirit among us, worship settles down into aesthetics, and varnishes and polishes the native human ego and pride of those who worship the work of their own hands or the sound of their own voices.

Margaret Montague writes about a hard-pressed woman who kept a picture of Christ in her bureau drawer. Time after time, when she seemed at the end of all her own resources, she would search out that picture. "What it did for her she never knew," she writes. She only knew "that she was in the presence of something transcendent, something bigger than she could ever touch, and yet which touched the biggest thing in herself."

The worship of the Christian church becomes supremely important when we become aware that we are in the presence of Him who is transcendent, the one Person who touches all of us at the deepest level of life.

And one reason Christian worship touches us at the deepest level is because it never lets us lose sight of the Man of five wounds, who suffered, died, and rose again—but all for us! As Augustine wrote, "The main cause of Christ's coming was that men might know how much God loves them."

What a difference it makes to know that Jesus is nothing less than our window into the heart of God. All through His life, Jesus was saying to men and women—and God was saying to men and women through Him—"This is the way I love you." When Jesus healed the sick and touched the untouchable, and loved the unlovely and the unlovable, God was saying, "This is the way I love you." When Peter denied and Judas betrayed, God was saying, "Nothing that any of you can do will ever make me stop loving you!" When Jesus prayed, "Father, forgive them, for they know not what they do," He was praying for us—all of us!

Because of his knowledge of the Risen Lord, Paul was able to sum it all up by saying, "I have become absolutely convinced that neither death nor life, neither messenger of Heaven nor monarch of earth, neither what happens today nor what may happen tomorrow, neither a power from on high nor a power from below, nor anything else in God's whole world has any power to separate us from the love of God in Jesus Christ our Lord!" (Rom. 8:38 Phillips). Amen.